D1315569

Sentence Tracing Practice Workbook

Sentence Handwriting Practice For Kindergarten And Grade 1 Kids

Printed by CreateSpace, An Amazon.com Company

SAMPLE PAGE

How To Use This Book:

This book contains 64 short and longer sentences for children to practise writing. First, the child will practise tracing the dotted words in the sentence for 7 times and then write out the words without the dots for 2 times and finally write one more time in the blank box provided without lines and dots. Each page gives the child 10 times of writing practice.

This is my teddy bear.

This is my teddy bear.

This is my teddy bear.

This is my teddy bear.

This is my teddy bear.

This is my teddy bear.

This is my teddy bear.

This is my teddy bear.

← Write without dots

← Write without dots

← Write the sentence inside the box without dots and lines

SAMPLE PAGE

Look at the bird.

Look at the bird.

Look at the bird.

Look at the bird.

Look at the bird.

Look at the bird.

Look at the bird.

Look at the bird.

SAMPLE PAGE

It is funny.

It is funny.

It is funny.

It is funny.

It is funny.

It is funny.

It is funny.

It is funny.

This is fun.

This is fun.

This is fun.

This is fun.

This is fun.

This is fun.

This is fun.

I like it.

I love it.

I love it.

I love it.

I love it.

I love it.

I love it.

I love it.

I love it.

I am happy.

I am happy.

I am happy.

I am happy.

I am happy.

I am happy.

I am happy.

I am sad.

I am sad.

I am sad.

I am sad.

I am sad.

I am sad.

I am sad.

I am sad.

I am excited

I am excited.

I am excited.

I am excited.

I am excited.

I am excited.

I am excited.

Look at me.

Look at me.

Look at me.

Look at me.

Look at me.

Look at me.

Look at me.

Look at me.

This is a chair.

This is a chair.

This is a chair.

This is a chair.

This is a chair.

This is a chair.

This is a chair.

This is a table.

This is a table.

This is a table.

This is a table.

This is a table.

This is a table.

This is a table.

This is my teddy bear.

This is my teddy bear.

This is my teddy bear.

This is my teddy bear.

This is my teddy bear.

This is my teddy bear.

This is my teddy bear.

This is my teddy bear.

Here is a flute.

Here is a drum.

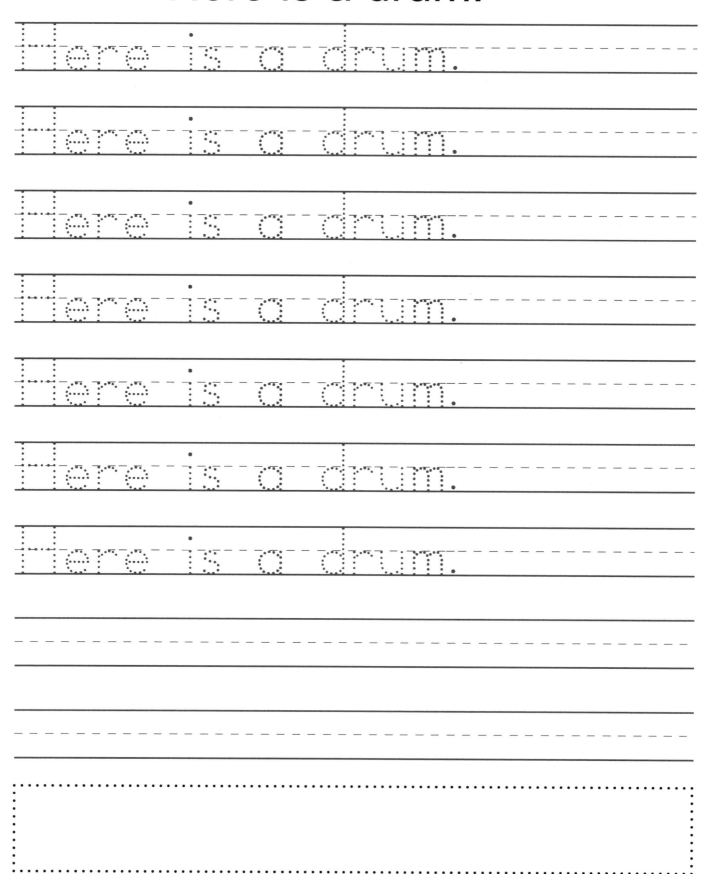

Here is a grasshopper.

Here is a grasshopper.

Here is a grasshopper.

Here is a grasshopper.

Here is a grasshopper.

Here is a grasshopper.

Here is a grasshopper.

Here is a red ball.

Here is a red ball.

Here is a red ball.

Here is a red ball.

Here is a red ball.

Here is a red ball.

Here is a red ball.

Here is a red ball.

Here is your hamburger.

Here is your hamburger.

Here is your hamburger.

Here is your hamburger.

Here is your hamburger.

Here is your hamburger.

Here is your hamburger.

Here is your hamburger.

Here is your toy car.

Here is your toy car.

Here is your toy car.

Here is your toy car.

Here is your toy car.

Here is your toy car.

Here is your toy car.

Here is your toy car.

We are at the zoo.

We are at the zoo.

We are at the zoo.

We are at the zoo.

We are at the zoo.

We are at the zoo.

We are at the zoo.

We are at the zoo.

I see a frog in the pond.

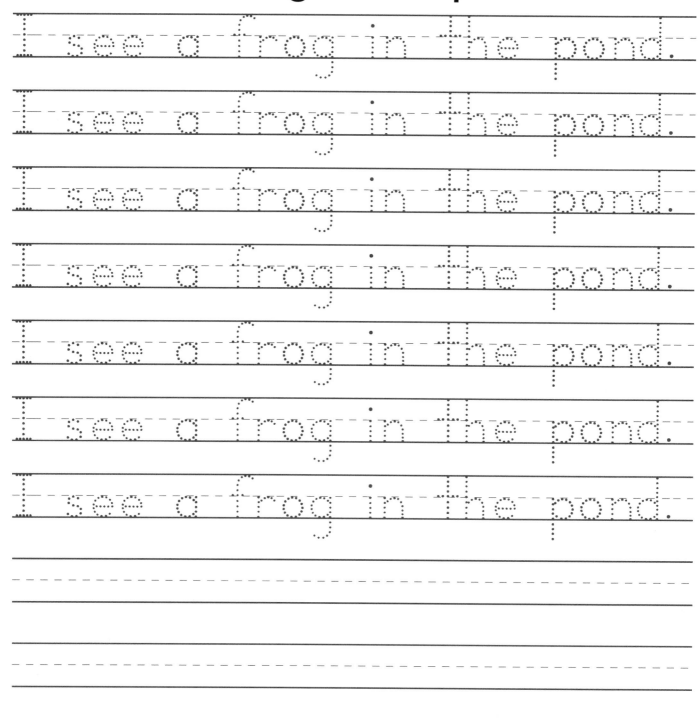

We went to the mall.

We went to the mall.

We went to the mall.

We went to the mall.

We went to the mall.

We went to the mall.

We went to the mall.

We went to the mall.

We went to the park.

We went to the park.

We went to the park.

We went to the park.

We went to the park.

We went to the park.

We went to the park.

We went to the park.

I can hop.

I can hop.

I can hop.

I can hop.

I can hop.

I can hop.

I can hop.

I can hop.

I know how to talk.

I know how to talk.

I know how to talk.

I know how to talk.

I know how to talk.

I know how to talk.

I know how to talk.

I know how to sing.

I know how to sing.

I know how to sing.

I know how to sing.

I know how to sing.

I know how to sing.

I know how to sing.

I can kick a ball.

I can kick a ball.

I can kick a ball.

I can kick a ball.

I can kick a ball.

I can kick a ball.

I can kick a ball.

I can kick a ball.

I can sing this song.

I can sing this song.

I can sing this song.

I can sing this song.

I can sing this song.

I can sing this song.

I can sing this song.

I can sing this song.

I love to play the drum.

I love to eat apples.

I love to eat apples.

I love to eat apples.

I love to eat apples.

I love to eat apples.

I love to eat apples.

I love to eat apples.

I love to eat apples.

I hear the bird sings.

I hear the bird sings.

I hear the bird sings.

I hear the bird sings.

I hear the bird sings.

I hear the bird sings.

I hear the bird sings.

I hear the bird sings.

I love to go to the park.

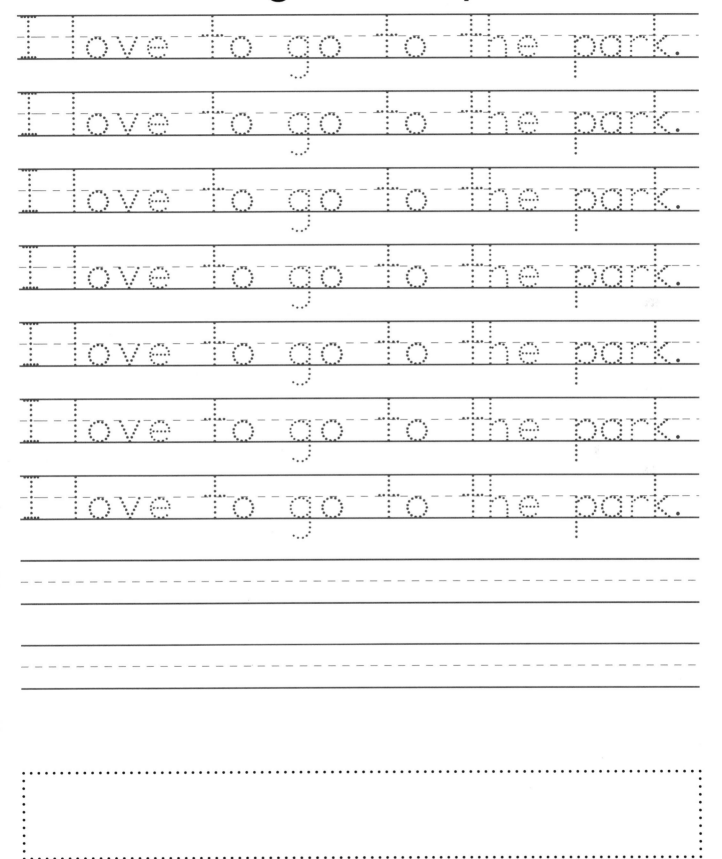

I love to ride in a train.

I love to ride in a train.

I love to ride in a train.

I love to ride in a train.

I love to ride in a train.

I love to ride in a train.

I love to ride in a train.

I love to ride in a train.

I love to sit on a swing.

I love to sit on a swing.

I love to sit on a swing.

I love to sit on a swing.

I love to sit on a swing.

I love to sit on a swing.

I love to sit on a swing.

I love to sit on a swing.

Look at the bird.

Look at the rabbit.

Look at the flower.

Look at the flower.

Look at the flower.

Look at the flower.

Look at the flower.

Look at the flower.

Look at the flower.

Look at the flower.

Look at that rainbow.

Look at that rainbow.

Look at that rainbow.

Look at that rainbow.

Look at that rainbow.

Look at that rainbow.

Look at that rainbow.

Look at that rainbow.

This is an aeroplane.

This is an aeroplane .

This is an aeroplane .

This is an aeroplane .

This is an aeroplane .

This is an aeroplane .

This is an aeroplane .

This is an aeroplane .

It is raining now.

It is raining now.

It is raining now.

It is raining now.

It is raining now.

It is raining now.

It is raining now.

It is a sunny day.

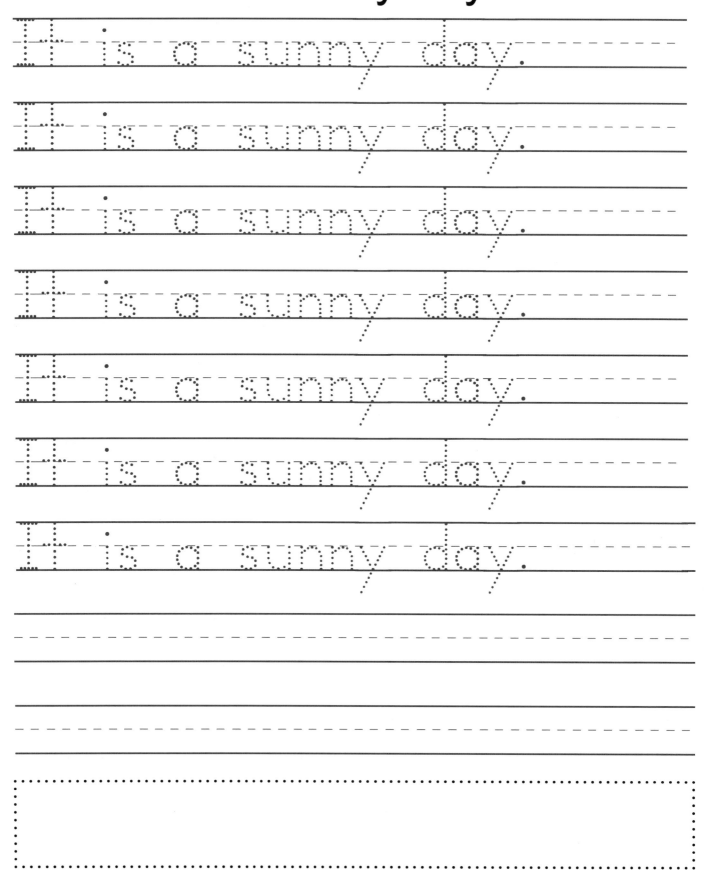

It is a wonderful day.

It is nice to meet you.

It is nice to meet you.

It is nice to meet you.

It is nice to meet you.

It is nice to meet you.

It is nice to meet you.

It is nice to meet you.

It is nice to meet you.

It is fun.

It is funny.

It is funny.

It is funny.

It is funny.

It is funny.

It is funny.

It is funny.

It is funny.

I am feeling happy.

I am feeling happy.

I am feeling happy.

I am feeling happy.

I am feeling happy.

I am feeling happy.

I am feeling happy.

I am feeling happy.

I am feeling sad.

I am feeling nervous.

I am feeling nervous.

I am feeling nervous.

I am feeling nervous.

I am feeling nervous.

I am feeling nervous.

I am feeling nervous.

I am feeling nervous.

Do you like animals?

Do you like animals?

Do you like animals?

Do you like animals?

Do you like animals?

Do you like animals?

Do you like animals?

Do you like animals?

Do you like pasta?

Do you like pasta?

Do you like pasta?

Do you like pasta?

Do you like pasta?

Do you like pasta?

Do you like pasta?

Do you like pasta?

Do you love swimming?

Do you love swimming?

Do you love swimming?

Do you love swimming?

Do you love swimming?

Do you love swimming?

Do you love swimming?

Do you love swimming?

Do you like fishing?

Do you like fishing?

Do you like fishing?

Do you like fishing?

Do you like fishing?

Do you like fishing?

Do you like fishing?

Do you like fishing?

I see the man walking.

I see the boy running.

I see the boy running.

I see the boy running.

I see the boy running.

I see the boy running.

I see the boy running.

I see the boy running.

I see the boy running.

I saw a brown bear.

I saw a brown bear.

I saw a brown bear.

I saw a brown bear.

I saw a brown bear.

I saw a brown bear.

I saw a brown bear.

I saw a tiger.

I saw a lizard.

I went to school.

I went to school.

I went to school.

I went to school.

I went to school.

I went to school.

I went to school.

I saw a butterfly.

I go to the playground.

I go to the playground.

I go to the playground.

I go to the playground.

I go to the playground.

I go to the playground.

I go to the playground.

I go to the playground.

I have a toy car.

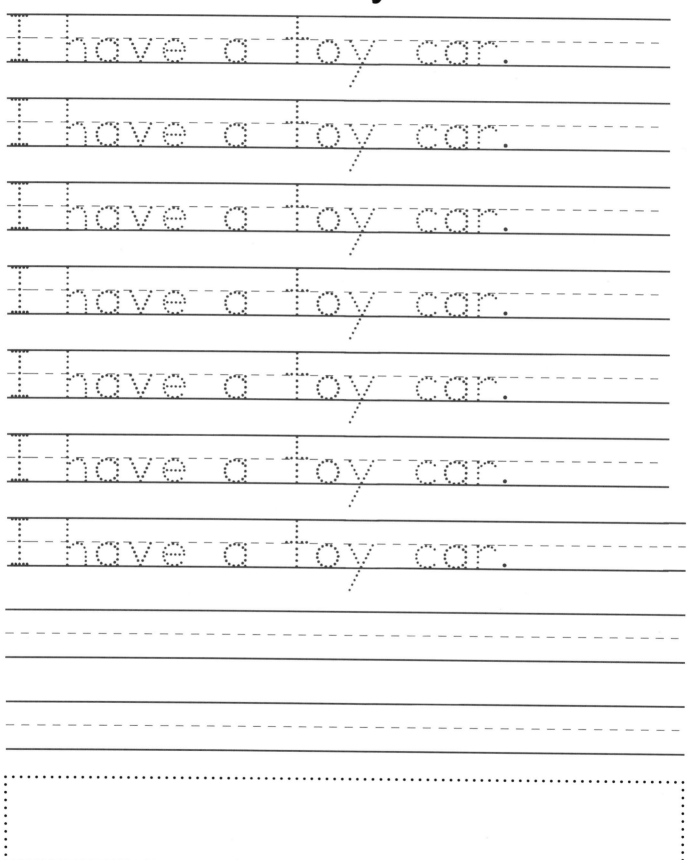

I have pasta for lunch.

I have pasta for lunch.

I have pasta for lunch.

I have pasta for lunch.

I have pasta for lunch.

I have pasta for lunch.

I have pasta for lunch.

I have pasta for lunch.

I like to watch movies.

I like to watch movies.

I like to watch movies.

I like to watch movies.

I like to watch movies.

I like to watch movies.

I like to watch movies.

I like to watch movies.

I feel happy.

I feel happy.

I feel happy.

I feel happy.

I feel happy.

I feel happy.

I feel happy.

I feel happy.

I feel great.

I ate an apple.

This is a big cat.

This is a big cat.

This is a big cat.

This is a big cat.

This is a big cat.

This is a big cat.

This is a big cat.

Made in the USA
Middletown, DE
09 June 2018